Lee

with thanks for

your wit + wisdom

and compliments

Michael

BREVITY IS THE SOUL OF WIT ... FOR WRITERS

A miscellany of memorable maxims

Curated by Michael J MacMahon

A book in the *Brevity Is the Soul* series

ALSO BY MICHAEL J MACMAHON

Back To The Black: how to become debt-free and stay that way

The Wedding Speech Handbook: how to make a great speech on the day it matters most

Brevity Is The Soul Of Wit, Vol. 1: a miscellany of mottos and maxims, an encyclopaedia of epigrams

This print edition 2023.
First published in Great Britain by Pembroke Media, 2023.

ISBN: 978-1-9993442-5-2

DEDICATION

"This is a florilegium, in which only the string binding the bouquet of flowers together is mine."

Those words were by Montaigne and are quoted in the wonderful *Writer's Commonplace Book* curated by Rosemary Friedman, to whom my thanks are due.

It is therefore dedicated to all my writer friends, in the hope that some of the quotations herein will be of use.

FOREWORD

Whenever fellow writers ask my advice about target word counts, I say, “As many words as your story needs - no more and no fewer”. Beginners are often surprised how quickly their manuscript shrinks when they remove superfluous words.

Such is the richness of our English language that even the shortest of sentences can convey a powerful message. I’m looking at you, EM Forster: “Only connect”.

Michael MacMahon’s collections of pithy quotations for different audiences epitomise the English aphorism. The volume you are reading now is the perfect gift for writers at any stage in their career, from nervous novices to seasoned bestsellers. The former, suffering from imposter syndrome, may take comfort from Adele Parks: “I believe writers are writers the day they describe themselves as such.” The latter, procrastinating before the blank page, will be spurred on by Thomas Jefferson: “It is wonderful how much may be done if we are always doing.” Thanks to this book, as I pen my thirteenth novel, that’s become my current writing mantra.

Which of Michael’s carefully curated words of wisdom for writers will you pin up over your desk? Read on and prepare to be inspired.

Debbie Young
www.authordebbieyoung.com

INTRODUCTION

Is this a dictionary? A comprehensive compilation? No, I don't aspire to either of those classifications. It is simply a collection of quotations that appeal to me and that I hope will be useful to writers. Subjectivity is inevitable in such an enterprise.

The book contains a selection of aphorisms, epigrams, mottos, maxims, quotations: all of those, and a few more too.

Aphorisms - and all those other descriptions - are by definition generalisations. And as we know, 'all generalisations are untrue, including this one.'

WHY DID I COMPILE THIS SERIES?

Two conversations, both a long way from my home and separated by several years, inspired me to start compiling the series of which this book forms a part.

The first was in Norway, at least ten years ago. I was having dinner with a colleague who became a good friend, management consultant Erle Bryn. Noticing that I had a photographic memory for quotations, she said 'you should publish a book of these things. And best of all, your friends would send you contributions.'

The second conversation was during a trip to Spain with my long-standing friend Tim Arnold. We've known each other since we played rugby together, and that was a very, very long time ago. However, we'd never spent several days together, so he'd not previously noticed my memory for quotations. That was a tendency that he thought weird. But then we're all weird in our own way.

Tim, being a marketing man to his bones, immediately came up with an idea. It wasn't for a book, but for a YouTube channel. Suiting action to the thought, he registered a channel for me while we sat in a Spanish bar.

As my Norwegian friend had predicted, friends and acquaintances did indeed send me contributions. And I shall shortly be opening my mailbox to contributions for further volumes.

AND WHAT'S A MOTTO?

My friend Tim suggested calling my YouTube channel 'The Mottoist.' I used to think that a motto was something you found in a Christmas cracker; but I was wrong. Consulting both Webster's and the Oxford English Dictionary, I found that it's another word for an aphorism, an epigram, a saying, a maxim, a tenet… you get the picture. So, with my newly acquired YouTube channel, I began to record mottos from time to time. And, as registered by Tim in that bar, the channel is indeed called The Mottoist.

SELECTION POLICY

This memory for pithy quotations is something I've always had. Some of my friends think this trait to be admirable; others, like Tim, find it weird.

Here you'll find mottos that I find inspirational or witty. You didn't think there was any method in my selection? But there is. The book contains quotations that either (a) represent my considered opinion at the time of editing (which might well change the following day), or (b) made me smile. Or, preferably, both.

COPYRIGHT ISSUES

For years, friends have been urging me to publish this kind of book. Also for years, I hesitated because I worried about copyright problems. Now I realise, not before time, that there are already scores of books of this type. The editors of such books simply could not have obtained permission from all the originators. So, as my extracts are all short, I rely on the principle of 'fair use' of material that has been previously published. If I have got that wrong, I hope you will send me food parcels.

ACKNOWLEDGEMENTS

Who are my sources?

If they are famous people, these quotations could have come from other anthologies, or from newspapers or magazines or online. So you might have seen them elsewhere.

However … in addition to sayings by famous people, I've also included things said to me by friends or family at some point in the last fifty years. Those you won't find anywhere else, obviously.

John Gross, Editor of The Oxford Book of Aphorisms, wrote 'like many anthologists, I owe a considerable debt to previous anthologies'. I echo his thanks.

Anyone publishing this kind of anthology might be accused of plagiarism. I know that 'stealing from one source is plagiarism, whereas stealing from many sources is research'. That truism has been known for centuries and was made memorable when set to music by Tom Lehrer in his song Lobachevsky.

So … thanks indeed to the compilers and publishers of other anthologies. Personal thanks are also due to Tim Arnold, John Lynch and Debbie Young; my late friends Erle Bryn and Phil Dunnington; and, of course, Tom Lehrer.

Finally, to my friend John Spencer Williams, to whom I am indebted for the idea of separate volumes for specific types of readers, such as this one.

CONTENTS

BATTLES OF THE SEXES, feat. LOVE AND MARRIAGE

"Try to avoid asking a writer who's also a woman any question that starts 'as a woman...'"

Emma Donoghue

"I would venture to guess that Anon, who wrote so many poems without signing them, was often a woman."

Virginia Woolf, *A Room of One's Own.* Excellent.

"To you I am neither man nor woman. I come before you as an author only. It is the sole standard by which you have a right to judge me--the sole ground on which I accept your judgment."

Charlotte Brontë

"Jane, I never meant to wound you thus...Will you ever forgive me?"

Reader, I forgave him at the moment and on the spot."

Charlotte Brontë, *Jane Eyre.* I always enjoy the 'fourth wall' device used in drama and recently revived by Phoebe Waller-

Bridge's TV series *Fleabag*. I didn't know that Charlotte Brontë had used the literary equivalent long ago.

‘CONTENT GENERATION’, AKA WRITING

“One forgets words as one forgets names. One’s vocabulary needs constant fertilisation or it will die.”

Evelyn Waugh. I intend to heed this warning. I used to pride myself on my memory; but as we know, pride comes before ...

“The arrow belongs not to the archer when it has once left the bow; the word no longer belongs to the speaker when it has once passed his lips.”

Heinrich Heine

“However fluent or witty your prose, it is simply no longer enough just to jump on a train.”

William Dalrymple. That’s a shame: why not, Mr Dalrymple? I like trains.

“There are things that get whispered about that writers are there to hear.”

Ann Beattie

"Never open a book with weather."

Elmore Leonard, *Ten rules for writing fiction.* Much as I love Mr Leonard's fiction, I have to take issue here. He was American, so maybe he didn't understand our fascination with weather forecasts.

"Show me a hero and I will write you a tragedy."

F Scott Fitzgerald

"It's useful to go out of this world and see it from the perspective of another one."

Terry Pratchett

"I think it is absolutely essential to have a notebook in your hands, always, and to scribble constantly."

William Dalrymple. I must remember to jot this down in my Moleskine.

"I could answer that a writer is someone who pays attention to the world."

Susan Sontag, from Edward Hirsch's *Susan Sontag, the art of fiction, no.143.* The more often I read this, the more I like it.

"Each has his past shut in him like the leaves of a book known to him by heart and his friends can only read the title."

Virginia Woolf. I loved this, though I'm lucky enough to have one or two friends who know my life and 'book' better than I do.

"Life can only be understood backwards; but it must be lived forwards."

Soren Kierkegaard

"I long ago became convinced that the most reliable source for arcane and obscure and seemingly unobtainable information does not lie with the government or law enforcement agencies. Apparently neither the CIA nor the military intelligence apparatus inside the Pentagon had even a slight inkling of the Soviet Union's impending collapse, right up to the moment the Kremlin's leaders were trying to cut deals for their memoirs with New York publishers. Or, if a person really wishes a lesson in the subjective nature of official information, he can always call the IRS and ask for help with his tax forms, then call back a half hour later and ask the same questions to a different representative. So where do you go to find a researcher who is intelligent, imaginative, skilled in the use of computers, devoted to discovering the truth, and knowledgeable about science, technology, history, and literature, and who usually works for dirt and gets credit for nothing? After lunch I drove to the city library on Main and asked the reference librarian to find what she could on Junior Crudup."

James Lee Burke, *Last Car to Elysian Fields.* We are lucky enough to have a fantastic central library where I live in Bristol. I'll deliver a copy of this paean to the librarians next time I'm there.

"If what one has to say is not better than silence, then one should keep silent."

Confucius. This advice should be made more widely available.

"Down these mean streets a man must go who is not himself mean, who is neither tarnished nor afraid. The detective must be a complete man and a common man and yet an unusual man. He must be, to use a rather weathered phrase, a man of honour."

Raymond Chandler. Maybe his most famous lines.

"It probably started in poetry; almost everything does."

Raymond Chandler

"A good title is the title of a successful book."

Raymond Chandler. I have shared this with a writer friend who says that Chandler (and Wodehouse) should be required reading in all our schools.

"One would think a writer would be happy here -- if a writer is ever happy anywhere."

Raymond Chandler, *The Long Goodbye.*

"The most durable thing in writing is style. It is a projection of personality and you have to have a personality before you can project it. It is the product of emotion and perception."

Raymond Chandler

“Had my books been any worse I would not have been invited to Hollywood and if they had been any better I would not have come.”

Raymond Chandler. I love this, so I’ve placed another copy in my ‘Wit and Wisdom’ section.

“The most durable thing in writing is style, and style is the single most valuable investment a writer can make with his time.”

Raymond Chandler

“The more you reason the less you create.”

Raymond Chandler

“Scarcely anything in literature is worth a damn except what is written between the lines.”

Raymond Chandler

“The actual writing is what you live for. The rest is something you have to get through in order to arrive at the point.”

Raymond Chandler

“The challenge is to write about real things magically.”

Raymond Chandler, *Selected Letters.*

“When I split an infinitive, God damn it, I split it so it will stay split.”

Raymond Chandler

“Don't ever write anything you don't like yourself and if you do like it, don't take anyone's advice about changing it. They just don't know.”

Raymond Chandler

“Throw up into your typewriter every morning. Clean up every noon.”

Raymond Chandler

“I'm of a fearsome mind to throw my arms around every living librarian who crosses my path, on behalf of the souls they never knew they saved.”

Barbara Kingsolver

“To my earlier self I would like to say, “Relax. The story will come in due time. Trust your characters. Let them tell you what happens next.”

Anne Tyler, *A Spool of Blue Thread.*

“I write because I want more than one life; I insist on a wider selection. It’s greed, plain and simple. When my characters join the circus, I’m joining the circus. Although I’m happily married, I spent a great deal of time mentally living with incompatible husbands.”

Anne Tyler

“It's true that writing is a solitary occupation, but you would be surprised at how much companionship a group of imaginary characters can offer once you get to know them.”

Anne Tyler

“One can often be in doubt about the effect of a word or a phrase, and one needs rules that one can rely on when instinct fails. I think the following rules will cover most cases:

1. Never use a metaphor, simile, or other figure of speech which you are used to seeing in print.
2. Never use a long word where a short one will do.
3. If it is possible to cut a word out, always cut it out.
4. Never use the passive where you can use the active.
5. Never use a foreign phrase, a scientific word, or a jargon word if you can think of an everyday English equivalent.
6. Break any of these rules sooner than say anything outright barbarous.”

George Orwell, *Politics and the English Language.*

“FICTION? I DON’T HAVE TIME TO READ FICTION”

“The truth is in the fiction.”

Martin Amis. He proved it to me, moreover: I wasn’t a big fan of his books until I read *The Zone Of Interest*, his fictionalised account that taught me more about Auschwitz than I’d ever understood before. And one day soon, if you and I are sitting over a drink, I’ll tell you what I learned about high-end gents’ tailoring from *The Tailor of Panama* by John le Carre. And if you’re still unconvinced, as I know many of my male friends will be, find and read *Stern Words To a Young Man Who Reads No Fiction*, a blog post by Richard Smith, former editor of the British Medical Journal who is one of the most prolific bloggers I know.

“Fiction is a physical confessional: when you’re within the covers of a book, you can admit to all kinds of things that you can’t otherwise.”

Joanna Trollope. Unlike the young man referenced by Richard Smith (see above), I do read fiction. But I don’t write it, so I have kept my comments to a minimum in this section.

“There is no longer any such thing as fiction and non-fiction; there’s only narrative.”

E L Doctorow

“The trouble with writing fiction is that it has to make sense, whereas real life doesn't.”

Iain Banks

“My brother-in-law wrote an unusual murder story. The victim was killed by a man from another book.”

Robert Sylvester. Love it!

“Having verse set to music is like looking at a painting through a stained glass window.”

Paul Valery. Much as I usually enjoy your stuff, Mr Valery, I don’t agree 100% with this. For example, have you heard the verse of John Betjeman, when read by the great man himself to the accompaniment of music by Jim Parker? Magical, IMHO.

“A poem is never finished; it’s always an accident that puts a stop to it - that is to say, gives it to the public.”

Paul Valery

"I do not believe that she wrote one word of fiction which does not put out boundaries a little way; one book which does not break new ground and form part of the total experiment."

Susan Hill, on Virginia Woolf.

"Contentment and fulfilment don't make for very good fiction."

Anthony Trollope

"Fiction is like a spider's web, attached ever so lightly perhaps, but still attached to life at all four corners."

Virginia Woolf, *A Room of One's Own.*

"But if you wanted to know what the retreat from Moscow really felt like, you wouldn't read a history of the Napoleonic wars – you'd read *War and Peace*."

Joanna Trollope

FILTHY LUCRE, AKA MONEY

"First I did it for my own pleasure. Then I did it for the pleasure of my friends and family. And now … now I do it for money."

Ferenc Molnar

"I loathe writing. On the other hand, I'm a great believer in money."

S J Perelman. He died more than 40 years ago but I've heard of him, so it's a fair guess that he made a living from his trade.

"The words I like are 'cheque' and 'enclosed.'"

Dorothy Parker, when asked about the most beautiful words in the English language.

IMPOSTER SYNDROME AND CRITICS

"Advice is seldom welcome; and those who want it the most always like it the least."

Philip, Lord Stanhope. I'm guessing that when the noble Lord wrote 'want it the most', he probably meant 'need' or 'lack' in our parlance.

"Unless a reviewer has the courage to give you unqualified praise, I say ignore the bastard."

John Steinbeck. I am on his side in this matter.

"I went for years not finishing anything because, of course, when you finish something you can be judged."

Erica Jong. She famously wrote *Fear of Flying*, presumably after conquering that other fear.

"Writers come in two principal categories: those who are overtly insecure and those who are covertly insecure. And they can all use help."

John McPhee

"On plenty of days the writer can write three or four pages, and on plenty of other days he concludes he must throw them all away."

Annie Dillard. Three or four whole pages, eh? A chance would be a fine thing.

"Once I have looked on it as completed … it becomes next to impossible to alter or amend. With the heavy suspicion on my mind that all may not be right, I yet feel forced to put up with the inevitably wrong."

Charlotte Brontë, to her editor. Could she too have suffered from the dreaded Imposter Syndrome?

"Asking a working writer what he thinks about critics is like asking a lamp-post how it feels about dogs."

Christopher Hampton

"A great deal of contemporary criticism reads to me like a man saying: 'Of course I do not like green cheese. I am very fond of brown sherry.'"

G K Chesterton. A wise man in this as in many other matters.

“I never read anything concerning my work. I feel that criticism is a letter to the public which the author, since it is not directed to him, does not have to open and read.”

Rainer Maria Rilke. Hear, hear! Messrs Rilke and Steinbeck (q.v.) are now my heroes.

“Writing criticism is to writing fiction and poetry as to hugging the shore is to sailing the open sea.”

John Updike. I’m no sailor but as a long-time Updike fan I’ll work it out. I trust that in matters nautical as well as others, he “knew stuff”, to quote Philip Roth, who added “I know nothing about anything.”

“It had only one fault. It was kind of lousy.”

James Thurber

“Critics! Appalled I venture on the name, those cut-throat bandits on the path to fame.”

Robert Burns

"A drama critic is a person who surprises the playwright by informing him what he meant."

Wilson Mizner. Brilliant.

"The greater part of critics are parasites who, if nothing had been written, would find nothing to write."

J B Priestley

"A critic is a man who knows the way but can't drive the car."

Kenneth Tynan, with one of the briefest and best descriptions of the genus.

"There is no such thing on earth as an uninteresting subject. The only thing that can exist is an uninterested person."

G K Chesterton. A late and dear friend of mine was a member of The Chesterton Society and I am belatedly discovering why he was.

"I've always been interested in people; but I've never liked them."

W Somerset Maugham. Wonderful; no doubt a soulmate of Philip Larkin.

“A cynic is a man who, when he smells flowers, looks around for a coffin.”

H L Mencken

“No one asked you to be happy. Get to work.”

Colette

“Fear is felt by writers at every level. Anxiety accompanies the first word they put on paper and the last.”

Ralph Keyes, *The courage to write: how writers transcend fear.*

“We’re professional worriers. You’re constantly imagining things that could go wrong and then writing about them.”

John Green, *The Late Late Show with Craig Ferguson.*

“I want to look like an American Voltaire or Gibbon but am slowly settling down to be a third-rate Boswell looking for a Dr Johnson.”

Henry Adams, from *Henry Adams, the major phase,* by Ernest Samuels.

“Worry doesn’t rob tomorrow of its sorrow but saps today of its strength.”

Is this about writing? I think it could apply to any creative enterprise at whose heels the dreaded Imposter Syndrome snaps regularly. I haven’t located the original originator, so will credit it with thanks to my friend Trish Roberts for providing it.

“Pay no attention to what the critics say. A statue has never been erected in honour of a critic.”

Jean Sibelius

INSPIRATION

"You never have to change anything you got up in the middle of the night to write."

Saul Bellow.

"At night, when the objective world has slunk back into its caverns and left dreamers to their own, there come inspirations and capabilities impossible at any less magical and quiet hour. No one knows whether or not he is a writer unless he has tried writing at night."

H P Lovecraft (1890 – 1937). I never knew you or your work, Mr Lovecraft, but your words have prompted me to try writing at night, which is something I never do.

"Decide when in the day (or night) it best suits you to write, and organise your life accordingly."

Andrew Motion. If our former Poet Laureate suggests this, maybe I should reevaluate my habits.

"Imagine thinking that black people write only about being black and not about being people."

Alice Walker

“And so when it’s difficult, what keeps me going is the possibility of joy.”

Chimamanda Ngozi Adichie, novelist and originator of the powerful TED talk *The Danger Of a Single Story.* (Growing up, she said: “I did not know that people like me could exist in literature.”)

“You can’t wait for inspiration. You have to go after it with a club.”

Jack London. Muscular motivation, as befits what I know about the man. As he was apparently one of the first Americans to make a fortune from writing, between an impoverished upbringing and his untimely death at 40, I should definitely follow his advice. And at least read some of his books.

“Your intuition knows what to write, so get out of the way.”

Ray Bradbury, one of my favourite sources for tips about writing.

“If one is lucky, a solitary fantasy can totally transform one million realities.”

Maya Angelou

"Imagination doesn't fall from the sky; you have to work with something."

Chimamanda Ngozi Adichie

"Imagination is more important than knowledge. For knowledge is limited to all we now know and understand, while imagination embraces the entire world, and all there ever will be to know and understand."

Albert Einstein, a man of many parts. A concert-level violinist!

"But it is when we have a story beating wildly deep inside in the chambers of our hearts, making us lose sleep at nights, asking to be born, demanding to be told, clawing at our flesh, a story stronger and wiser and ultimately better than our deeply flawed selves, that is when we start to become a writer."

Elif Shafak

"Therefore I would ask you to write all kinds of books, hesitating at no subject however trivial or however vast. By hook or by crook, I hope that you will possess yourselves of money enough to travel and to idle, to contemplate the future or the past of the world, to dream over books and loiter at street corners and let the line of thought dip deep into the stream."

Virginia Woolf, *A Room of One's Own.* What a wonderful wish!

"So long as you write what you wish to write, that is all that matters; and whether it matters for ages or only for hours, nobody can say."

Virginia Woolf, *A Room of One's Own.*

"Lock up your libraries if you like; but there is no gate, no lock, no bolt that you can set upon the freedom of my mind."

Virginia Woolf, *A Room of One's Own.* A timely reminder, in a Britain where local councils are trying to save insignificant amounts by closing these valuable spaces, staffed by librarians who are paid pennies for their skills. (as attested by James Lee Burke, q.v.)

"E. L. Doctorow once said that writing a novel is like driving a car at night. You can see only as far as your headlights, but you can make the whole trip that way. This is right up there with the best advice about writing, or life, I have ever heard."

Anne Lamott, *Bird by Bird: Instructions on Writing and Life.* A writer quoting another writer: epigram gold.

"The privilege of a lifetime is to become who you really are."

Carl Jung

"To talk to each other is but a more animated and an audible thinking."

Charlotte Brontë, *Jane Eyre.*

"I became a journalist because I did not want to rely on newspapers for information."

Christopher Hitchens, *my hero.*

“A writer who is afraid to overreach himself is as useless as a general who is afraid to be wrong.”

Raymond Chandler, *Pearls are a Nuisance.* Is this a realistic analogy? But it’s Chandler, so I included it anyway.

“There are two kinds of truth: the truth that lights the way and the truth that warms the heart. The first of these is science, and the second is art. Neither is independent of the other or more important than the other. Without art science would be as useless as a pair of high forceps in the hands of a plumber. Without science art would become a crude mess of folklore and emotional quackery. The truth of art keeps science from becoming inhuman, and the truth of science keeps art from becoming ridiculous."

Raymond Chandler, *The Notebooks of Raymond Chandler; and English Summer: A Gothic Romance.*

“If we can't, as artists, improve on real life, we should put down our pencils and go bake bread.”

Barbara Kingsolver

"Close the door. Write with no one looking over your shoulder. Don't try to figure out what other people want to hear from you; figure out what you have to say. It's the one and only thing you have to offer."

Barbara Kingsolver. One of the best pieces of writing advice I've ever read.

"The book that made me want to be a writer was John Steinbeck's *Cannery Row*. I'd written privately since childhood, but never imagined writing for anyone else, because I didn't know anything important. Then in my mid-20s I read a funny, beautiful novel about an odd little scramble of not-important people. I thought: "I could try to write a book like that," and I did. It was *The Bean Trees*."

Barbara Kingsolver. I have long belonged to the fan-club for *Cannery Row*. And, subsequently, for Ms Kingsolver.

"What's the point of living if you don't try to do things better?"

Anne Tyler. Said by a character in Redhead by the Side of the Road. So there's a good chance that this is Ms Tyler's own attitude, which makes me like her even more.

"But sometimes, very occasionally, songs and books and films and pictures express who you are perfectly. And they don't do this in words or images, necessarily; the connection is a lot less direct and more complicated than that. When I was first beginning to write seriously, I read Anne Tyler's Dinner at the Homesick Restaurant, and suddenly knew what I was, and what I wanted to be, for better or worse. It's a process something like falling in love. You don't necessarily choose the best person, or the wisest, or the most beautiful; there's something else going on. There was a part of me that would rather have fallen for Updike or Kerouac, or DeLillo – for someone masculine, or at least, maybe somebody a little more opaque, and certainly someone who uses more swearwords- and, though I have admired those writers, at various stages in my life, admiration is a very different thing from the kind of transference I'm talking about. I'm talking about understanding – or at least feeling like I understand- every artistic decision, every impulse, the soul of both the work and its creator. "This is me," I wanted to say when I read Tyler's rich, sad, lovely novel. "I'm not a character, I'm nothing like the author, I haven't had the experiences she writes about. But even so, this is what I feel like, inside. This is what I would sound like, if I ever I were to find a voice." And I did find a voice, eventually, and it was mine, not hers; but nevertheless, so powerful was the process of identification that I still don't feel as though I've expressed myself as well, as completely, as Tyler did on my behalf."

Nick Hornby, *Songbook.* He has clearly joined the swelling numbers of the Tyler fan-club. Not brief; but I like it.

"If I waited till I felt like writing, I'd never write at all."

Anne Tyler. If that's truthful, then her output is even more impressive. This admission also appears in my Work Ethic section.

"Words can be like X-rays if you use them properly – they'll go through anything. You read and you're pierced."

Aldous Huxley, *Brave New World. Wow.*

"The more powerful and original a mind, the more it will incline towards the religion of solitude."

Aldous Huxley. After reading this I am trying to adopt a solitary life, so as to join the ranks of the powerful and original minds.

"Every man's memory is his private literature."

Aldous Huxley

"The trouble with fiction," said John Rivers, "is that it makes too much sense. Reality never makes sense."

Aldous Huxley, *The Genius And The Goddess.* Reminds me of a statement by Julian Barnes in *Flaubert's Parrot:* "Books say she did this because … but life says she did this."

"A scrupulous writer, in every sentence that he writes, will ask himself at least four questions, thus: 1. What am I trying to say? 2. What words will express it? 3. What image or idiom will make it clearer? 4. Is this image fresh enough to have an effect?"

George Orwell, *Politics and the English Language.* I've also included Orwell's famous six rules, q.v.

"I have no idea what I am doing but incompetence has never prevented me from plunging in with enthusiasm."

Woody Allen

"Writing a book is a horrible, exhausting struggle, like a long bout with some painful illness. One would never undertake such a thing if one were not driven on by some demon whom one can neither resist nor understand."

George Orwell

“If you're not failing every now and again, it's a sign you're not doing anything very innovative.”

Woody Allen, in serious mode. Who knew that could happen?

“The finest fury is the most controlled.”

Christopher Hitchens, *Love, Poverty, and War: Journeys and Essays.* A dictum whose truth he demonstrated countless times. Good advice for anyone planning to write a polemic, or to enter politics.

“Misunderstanding is my cornerstone. It's everyone's, come to think of it. Illusions mistaken for truth are the pavement under our feet.”

Barbara Kingsolver, *The Poisonwood Bible*

“Imitation is not just the sincerest form of flattery - it's the sincerest form of learning.”

George Bernard Shaw

"Reading made Don Quixote a gentleman. Believing what he read made him mad."

George Bernard Shaw

"Life is no brief candle to me. It is a sort of splendid torch which I have got a hold of for the moment, and I want to make it burn as brightly as possible before handing it on to future generations."

George Bernard Shaw

"This is the true joy in life, the being used for a purpose recognized by yourself as a mighty one; the being thoroughly worn out before you are thrown on the scrap heap; the being a force of Nature instead of a feverish selfish little clod of ailments and grievances complaining that the world will not devote itself to making you happy."

George Bernard Shaw

"No one is useless in this world who lightens the burdens of another."

Charles Dickens. I think George Eliot said something very similar, speaking of Dorothea Brooke probably, in *Middlemarch.* I can recall writers who have lightened my own burdens on more than one occasion. And I hope you can too.

"And yet, the only exciting life is the imaginary one."

Virginia Woolf

“You often come across the best stories when you least expect them.”

William Dalrymple

"Every secret of a writer's soul, every experience of his life, every quality of his mind is written large in his works.'

Virginia Woolf

"Reading any piece of writing aloud is an acid test, particularly when it comes to dialogue. There were writers I'd always admired who suddenly rang false when I spoke their words in our living room."

Anne Tyler

“I read so I can live more than one life in more than one place”

Anne Tyler. She also said (q.v.) that this is why she writes.

KNOWLEDGE, DISCOVERY

"I've seen how you can't learn anything when you're trying to look like the smartest person in the room."

Barbara Kingsolver, *The Poisonwood Bible.* I love this. Reminds me of two things: the movie about the collapse of Enron was called *The Smartest Guys In the Room;* and a remark by an Israeli negotiator at the Oslo Peace Accord negotiations: "we are not here to prove who is the smartest guy in the room; we are here to find solutions." Oh and the famous quote by Confucius, who said that if you actually are the smartest person in the room, you're in the wrong room. To which Ms Kingsolver would probably agree.

"Close the door. Write with no one looking over your shoulder. Don't try to figure out what other people want to hear from you; figure out what you have to say. It's the one and only thing you have to offer."

Barbara Kingsolver

"You cannot open a book without learning something."

Confucius. Well, I'm not so sure. I once started to read a book by.... But my lips are sealed, as you might be a fan of that author's work.

"It is the mark of an educated mind to be able to entertain a thought without accepting it."

Aristotle

"The book I reread was George Eliot's *Middlemarch*. I reread it at least once per decade, because it's about everything, for every person, at every age."

Barbara Kingsolver. *Hear, hear!*

"If people cannot write well, they cannot think well, and if they cannot think well, others will do their thinking for them."

George Orwell. Not from one of his novels, as far as I know. A chilling thought.

"Two percent of the people think; three percent of the people think they think; and ninety-five percent of the people would rather die than think."

George Bernard Shaw. Reminds me of Henry Ford: "Thinking is the hardest work there is, which is why so few people engage in it."

PLAGIARISM, QUOTATIONS AND COPYRIGHT

"If you steal from one book you are condemned as a plagiarist. But if you steal from ten books you are considered a scholar; and if you steal from thirty or forty books, a distinguished scholar."

Amos Oz

"Immature poets imitate; mature poets steal."

T S Eliot

"We can say nothing but what has been said. Our poets steal from Homer. Our story-dressers do as much; he that comes last is commonly best."

Robert Burton *(1577-1640)*

"They lard their lean books with the fat of others' works."

Robert Burton *(1577-1640)*

"Plagiarise! Plagiarise, plagiarise, plagiarise. Let no-one else's work evade your eyes …. only be sure always to call it research."

Tom Lehrer, *Lobachevsky.* Stealing from many sources is called research: that truism has been known for centuries but was made memorable in the 1950s when set to music by Harvard mathematics professor Tom Lehrer in this comic song.

"Famous remarks are seldom quoted correctly."

Simeon Strunsky

"The highest compliment you can pay a writer is to misquote him. It means that his work has become a part of our mind and not merely of our library."

G. K. Chesterton

"The secret to creativity is knowing how to hide your sources."

Albert Einstein. The legendary polymath evidently had a sense of humour too.

“Independence? That's middle class blasphemy. We are all dependent on one another, every soul of us on earth.”

George Bernard Shaw. I justify including this in a book for writers, to remind me that we are all influenced by what we read, so the existence of a truly original thought is a rarity. Maybe too, I hope, it’s a counter-statement to Margaret Thatcher’s famous dictum “There’s no such thing as society.”

PLOTTING VERSUS 'PANTSING'

"Writing tends to be very deliberate. A novelist could probably run a military campaign with some success. They could certainly run a country."

Colm Toibin. Now I know why I don't write novels: I would be useless running a military campaign. But running the country, on the other hand ...

"If you write about a dog and the dog dies, you are in trouble."

Matt Haig, 25 *rules for writing a novel.* I can't improve on this.

"In writing a novel, when in doubt, have two guys come through the door with guns."

Raymond Chandler. I don't write novels but if I did, I would follow all of Mr Chandler's advice.

RANDOM PUT-DOWNS

"Literature is an occupation in which you have to keep proving you have talent to people who have none."

Jules Renard. Harsh on critics? I like lots of Mr Renard's stuff, so I'll take this as the fruit of experience.

"My God, what a clumsy olla putrida James Joyce is! Nothing but old fags and cabbage stumps of quotations from the Bible and the rest, stewed in the juice of deliberate, journalistic dirty-mindedness."

D H Lawrence. As I am currently struggling through *Ulysses* (I'm part-Irish, so I always felt I should), maybe this from Lawrence is a sufficient excuse to give up the unequal struggle.

"English literature's performing flea."

Sean O'Casey, on P G Wodehouse. Had to include this to balance my own almost unlimited admiration for PGW. I'll give O'Casey the benefit of the doubt: maybe a bad hangover prompted this bilious attack.

“If you think … that anything like a romance is preparing for you, reader, you were never more mistaken. Do you anticipate sentiment, and poetry, and reverie? Do you expect passion, and stimulus, and melodrama? Calm your expectations, reduce them to a lowly standard. Something real, cool and solid lies before you; something as unromantic as Monday morning, when all who have work wake with the consciousness that they must rise and betake themselves thereto.

Charlotte Brontë, Prelude to *Shirley.* Recycled with thanks to David Lodge. He used this quotation as an introduction to his 1988 novel *Nice Work,* which was largely about the world of Monday mornings.

I add this to my ‘random put-downs’ section, as befits this wonderful example of that most English type of humour, i.e. self-deprecation.

“The trouble with her is that she lacks the power of conversation but not the power of speech.”

George Bernard Shaw. Ouch! I am happy to include such an example of Shavian acidity, as I don’t know to whom he was referring.

"Fate has not been kind to Mrs Browning. Nobody reads her, nobody discusses her, nobody troubles to put her in her place."

Virginia Woolf, brilliant as ever, on Elizabeth Barrett Browning.

"Oh God. I can't bear Sebastian Faulks. It's just Mills and Boon with guns!"

Isabel Wolff. As I like Sebastian Faulks and had never heard of Ms Wolff, I had to check her out. According to Wikipedia, she is a chick-lit novelist based in London, "who also has a home on the Roseland Peninsula." That's in the South-West of England. They didn't say much else, so I shall retain my liking for Mr Faulks.

"It is not long since the grave closed over George Eliot, or more properly speaking, Mary Ann Evans, and yet it has already been faintly been whispered by some, and loudly asserted by others, that she has been greatly overrated."

Julia Clara Byrne. I include this calumny for the sake of balance. And will defend the right of Ms Byrne (who she?) to hold that opinion, by saying that if the said grave had "not long since closed", we ourselves have had the benefit of time and perspective to consider Ms Eliot's position as one of the greatest of English novelists. A claim that I shall assert and defend, despite having only recently become a fan. Her *Middlemarch* is now my favourite novel. But I am only 79, so I have time to change my mind.

"The truth is, everyone likes to look down on someone. If your favourites are all avant-garde writers who throw in Sanskrit and German, you can look down on everyone. If your favourites are all Oprah Book Club books, you can at least look down on mystery readers. Mystery readers have sci-fi readers. Sci-fi can look down on fantasy. And yes, fantasy readers have their own snobbishness. I'll bet this, though: in a hundred years, people will be writing a lot more dissertations on Harry Potter than on John Updike. Look, Charles Dickens wrote popular fiction. Shakespeare wrote popular fiction—until he wrote his sonnets, desperate to show the literati of his day that he was real artist. Edgar Allan Poe tied himself in knots because no one realized he was a genius. The core of the problem is how we want to define 'literature'. The Latin root simply means 'letters'. Those letters are either delivered—they connect with an audience—or they don't. For some, that audience is a few thousand college professors and some critics. For others, it's twenty million women desperate for romance in their lives. Those connections happen because the books successfully communicate something real about the human experience. Sure, there are trashy books that do really well, but that's because there are trashy facets of humanity. What people value in their books—and thus what they count as literature—really tells you more about them than it does about the book."

Brent Weeks. I hope he's wrong about Harry Potter versus John Updike but I liked this, even if it's not brief.

"Jane Austen's novels, which strangely retain their hold on the public taste, are tedious to those who dare to think for themselves."

Kate Sanborn, American author around the start of the 20th century. I include this only as a warning to my author friends that the fame and acclaim you will certainly achieve might not insulate one from the occasional barb: on the contrary, it might encourage such barbs. And a reminder of the old saying 'everyone to their own taste'.

"There are books of which the backs and covers are by far the best parts."

Charles Dickens, *Oliver Twist.* Said at a time when most books had really basic covers, so it was especially harsh.

READING AND WRITING

"A lonesome man on a rainy day who does not know how to read."

Benjamin Franklin, on being asked what condition of man he considered the most pitiable. We have many rainy days in the UK and I like to spend some time in solitude, so this gem reminds me always to carry reading material.

"Read, read, read. I'm not sure that one can be a good writer without being a good reader. If you're going to build a desk it's very good to see what other carpenters have done."

Chimamanda Ngozi Adichie. Great analogy.

"At last, an unprintable book that is worth reading."

Ezra Pound, on Henry Miller's *Tropic of Cancer.* Now I have to read it.

"If a book is worth reading, it is worth buying."

John Ruskin, in an encomium for the bookselling business.

“Any novel is hopeful in that it presupposes a reader.”

Margaret Atwood, whose presuppositions were always well-founded.

“Try to read your own work as if you didn’t write it. As if you are a reader coming to it for the first time.”

David Lodge. Good advice. I’ve often had a parallel experience, coming upon something I’d forgotten writing many years previously. So my judgment is probably untrammelled by the dreaded Imposter Syndrome. In such situations I always admire my own writing.

“The reading of all good books is like a conversation with the finest men of past centuries.”

Rene Descartes.

“Reading maketh a full man; conference a ready man; and writing an exact man.”

Francis Bacon

"Reading is always a good way to define pleasure anew."

Richard Ford. At first I thought that this was the American novelist who is one of my very favourite contemporary writers. But that word 'anew' gave me pause, so I checked. There was an earlier man of that name, a 19th-century English travel writer. Sadly, my friend Mr Google was no help on the matter.

"There are two motives for reading a book. One, that you enjoy it; the other, that you can boast about it."

Bertrand Russell. I didn't know that Russell had such a sense of humour in addition to his manifold other talents. Must start reading him.

"When a man writes from his own mind, he writes very rapidly. The greatest part of a writer's time is spent in reading, in order to write; a man will turn over half a library to make one book."

Samuel Johnson. I love this description of the process.

"A library is thought in cold storage."

Herbert Samuel. An elegant and topical observation.

“I love to lose myself in other men’s minds. When I am not walking, I am thinking; I cannot sit and think. Books think for me.”

Charles Lamb

“I’m also a believer in reading what you dislike at least once, just to know.”

Chimamanda Ngozi Adichie. OK, if you insist, Ms Adichie.

“Language is the autobiography of the human mind.”

Max Müller.

"But then anyone who's worth anything reads just what he likes, as the mood takes him, and with extravagant enthusiasm."

Virginia Woolf

"I am reading six books at once, the only way of reading; since, as you will agree, one book is only a single unaccompanied note, and to get the full sound, one needs ten others at the same time."

Virginia Woolf, *The Letters of Virginia Woolf: Volume Three,* 1923-1928. Now I feel better about my own undisciplined reading habits. I too like "the full sound", so if it was good enough for Ms Woolf, it's good enough for me.

"When the Day of Judgment dawns and people, great and small, come marching in to receive their heavenly rewards, the Almighty will gaze upon the mere bookworms and say to Peter, "Look, these need no reward. We have nothing to give them. They have loved reading."

Virginia Woolf.

"I learned to write by reading the kind of books I wished I'd written."

Barbara Kingsolver. I seem to remember that *Cannery Row* (q.v.) was one such book.

"Originality is nothing but judicious imitation. The most original writers borrowed one from another. The instruction we find in books is like fire. We fetch it from our neighbour's, kindle it at home, communicate it to others, and it becomes the property of all."

Voltaire. "Judicious imitation?" Should this be in my section on plagiarism? Perhaps it already is.

"You cannot open a book without learning something."

Confucius. On the other hand ...

"I cannot live without books."

Thomas Jefferson

"The man who reads nothing at all is better educated than the man who reads nothing but newspapers."

Thomas Jefferson. I've seen various versions of this and they vary slightly in their wording. I have friends who are wedded to keeping abreast of the news as presented by their favourite newspapers; and don't read much else. Shall I show them this quotation? Probably not, as I value their friendship.

"With my book in one hand

And my drink in the other

What more could I want

But fame,

Better health,

And ten million dollars?"

Kenneth Burke. Yet another Burke; unconnected with the others. I didn't know this one but my friend Wikipedia tells me that he was a serious thinker who also had a witty turn of phrase:

"Kenneth Duva Burke was an American literary theorist, as well as poet, essayist, and novelist, who wrote on 20th-century philosophy, aesthetics, criticism, and rhetorical theory. As a literary theorist, Burke was best known for his analyses based on the nature of knowledge."

"I get sad every time I hear a person say 'I don't read.' It's like saying 'I don't learn,' or 'I don't laugh,' or 'I don't live.'"

Alafair Burke, lawyer, best-selling crime writer and the daughter of my favourite contemporary crime writer, James Lee Burke. Her dad brought her up well, I'd say.

“The greatest gift is a passion for reading.”

Edmund Burke

“Reading without reflecting is like eating without digesting.”

Edmund Burke. OK, this is about reading, not writing. But all the writers I know are avid readers too.

“Reading made Don Quixote a gentleman. Believing what he read made him mad.”

George Bernard Shaw

“If there was graffiti in a lavatory cubicle, I had to read every word, and sometimes even corrected the spelling and punctuation.”

Sue Townsend. Most writers are avid readers; but was this going a little too far? Discuss.

“I was a print slut. I would read anything, anytime, anywhere: The Beano, the Spectator and the Kellogg’s cereal packet.”

Sue Townsend. Good to know I wasn’t the only one.

"Read widely and with discrimination. Bad writing is contagious."

P D James. *Ten rules for writing fiction, The Guardian, 2010.*

BUT …

"One should accept bad writing as a way of priming the pump, a warm-up exercise that allows you to write well."

Jennifer Egan

AND

"I'm also a believer in reading what you dislike at least once, just to know."

Chimamanda Ngozi Adichie

RECOGNITION

"It is not enough to succeed. Others must fail."

Gore Vidal.

"Few people think more than two or three times a year; I have made an international reputation for myself by thinking once or twice a week."

George Bernard Shaw

"If by the people you mean the multitude, the hoi polloi, 'tis no matter what they think. They are sometimes in the right, sometimes in the wrong. Their judgment is a mere lottery."

John Dryden. *No less true today than in the 17th century.*

"The worst thing that can happen to a writer is to become a Writer."

Mary McCarthy. Very good! I love this because I have no aspiration to become a Writer.

"Those who have succeeded at anything and don't mention luck are kidding themselves."

Larry King, legendary US talk-show host who died recently. He interviewed every sitting US president, countless showbiz and sports celebrities and thousands of members of the public who phoned in to his show. His point was developed in the book *Outliers* by Malcolm Gladwell.

RUBBISH FIRST DRAFTS

"There is no such thing as good writing, only good rewriting."

Robert Graves

"Any story that is any good is usually going to change."

Alice Munro

"The second draft is where I try to make it look as if I knew what I was doing all along."

Neil Gaiman. There are so many quotations about rubbish first drafts but this is my favourite.

"Looking back, I imagine I was always writing. Twaddle it was too. But better by far to write twaddle or anything, anything, than nothing at all."

Katherine Mansfield

"Put down everything that comes into your head and then you're a writer. But an author is one who can judge his own stuff's worth, without pity, and destroy most of it."

Colette

"I'm a great believer in chaos. I don't believe that you start with a formula and then you fulfil the formula."

Sam Shepard

"On plenty of days the writer can write three or four pages, and on plenty of other days he concludes he must throw them all away."

Annie Dillard. I might have entered this into another category: not sure. Three or four pages, eh? One page will do me today.

"Get it down. Take chances. It may be bad but it's the only way you can do anything really good."

William Faulkner

"The first draft is just you telling yourself the story."

Terry Pratchett

"Get it all down. Let it pour out of you and onto the page. Write an incredibly shitty, self-indulgent, whiny, mewling first draft. Then take out as many of the excesses as you can."

Anne Lamott, *Bird by bird: some instructions on writing and life.* I hate the word shitty but it's OK here, because it's someone else saying it. And I like Ms Lamott's attitudes.

"Every first draft is perfect, because all a first draft has to do is exist."

Jane Smiley

"Don't hold on to poor work. If it was bad when it went into the drawer, it will be just as bad when it comes out."

Jeanette Winterson

“It takes a lot of bad writing to get to a little good writing.”

Truman Capote.

"I know some very great writers, writers you love who write beautifully and have made a great deal of money, and not one of them sits down routinely feeling wildly enthusiastic and confident. Not one of them writes elegant first drafts. All right, one of them does, but we do not like her very much."

Anne Lamott, *Bird by Bird: Instructions on Writing and Life. Ha!*

"Practically even better news than that of short assignments is the idea of shitty first drafts. All good writers write them. This is how they end up with good second drafts and terrific third drafts."

Anne Lamott, *Bird by Bird: Instructions on Writing and Life.*

“Finishing a book is like taking a small child out into the yard and shooting it.”

Truman Capote. Famous and depressing words.

“On matters of style, swim with the current, on matters of principle, stand like a rock.”

Thomas Jefferson

“Editors are super-smart, the only people smart enough to understand how stupid and shallow the readers are.”

Alice Kahn

“I saw editors as the people who cut all the good stuff out of my stories.”

Alice Kahn. Nowadays we’re often enjoined to “kill your darlings” but that has always been the job of the editor.

“Any intelligent fool can make things bigger, more complex, and more violent. It takes a touch of genius — and a lot of courage to move in the opposite direction.”

E.F. Schumacher, *Small Is Beautiful: Economics as if People Mattered.* An endorsement of the editor’s craft.

SELL BOOKS? I'D RATHER JUST WRITE THEM. EDITING, MARKETING AND ALL THAT

"You have to know how to accept rejection and reject acceptance."

Ray Bradbury

"It's a formula-driven business. If you've written one book about a bricklayer, they want you to write 1,000 books about a bricklayer."

Dean Koontz. A chance would be a fine thing. Not that I've ever written a book about a bricklayer.

"Some writers enjoy writing. Not me. I enjoy having written."

George R R Martin. This is perfect. It is me.

"An editor is one who separates the wheat from the chaff and prints the chaff."

Adlai Stevenson

"To write books is easy, it requires only pen and ink and the ever-patient paper. To print books is a little more difficult, because genius so often rejoices in illegible handwriting. To read books is more difficult still, because of a tendency to go to sleep. But the most difficult task of all that a mortal man can embark on is to sell a book."

Stanley Unwin. Most of the writers that I know will say "hear, hear!"

"Your manuscript is your baby, maybe your only child, but your publisher finds a dozen or so new babies on his doorstep every morning and has several thousand older children over-running his warehouse and his entire establishment, all of them calling simultaneously for his undivided attention."

Stanley Unwin, *Writers' & Artists' Yearbook 1950.* Wise words from the legendary 'Professor' Unwin. Maybe a good argument for self-publishing?

"This manuscript of yours that has just come back from another editor is a precious package. Don't consider it rejected. Consider that you've addressed it 'to the editor who can appreciate my work' and it has simply come back stamped 'Not at this address'. Just keep looking for the right address."

Barbara Kingsolver. Brilliant way of putting it.

“We don’t want literature, my friend. We want a best-seller.”

Anthony Burgess

“Publishing is a marketplace, not a meritocracy.”

Alice Kahn

THE DEMON DRINK

"Sober or blotto, this is your motto. Keep muddling through."

P G Wodehouse, *A Damsel In Distress*. A quote that I dedicate to my good friend Tim Arnold, who was a major part of the inspiration for this book when he registered a YouTube channel for me entitled *The Mottoist;* and with whom I've spent many a pleasant hour: if not exactly blotto, then certainly not sober.

"It has become increasingly plain to me that the very excellent organisation of a long book or the finest perceptions and judgment in time of revision do not go well with liquor."

F Scott Fitzgerald.

AND ...

"No alcohol, sex or drugs while you are working."

Colm Toibin, *Ten rules for writing fiction, part 2.*

ON THE OTHER HAND …

“Write when drunk but edit when sober.”

Christopher Hitchens

“Between the study and the bed, liquor stands me in good stead.”

Attribution unclear, at least to me. A character in a Julian Barnes novel (I forget which one) comes out with these words. I memorised them but have been unable to trace their origin... even with the aid of Google. But according to *The Thirties*: *From Notebooks and Diaries of the Period*, by Edmund Wilson, Tolstoy might have been the source. In which case I’d also happily credit the translator, if I only knew who he or she was.

THE HUMAN CONDITION

“I became a journalist because I did not want to rely on newspapers for information.”

Christopher Hitchens

“[Raymond Chandler] wrote as if pain hurt and life mattered.”

The New Yorker

“The French have a phrase for it. The bastards have a phrase for everything and they are always right. To say goodbye is to die a little.”

Raymond Chandler, *The Long Goodbye.*

“We were keeping our eye on 1984. When the year came and the prophecy didn't, thoughtful Americans sang softly in praise of themselves. The roots of liberal democracy had held. Wherever else the terror had happened, we, at least, had not been visited by Orwellian nightmares.

But we had forgotten that alongside Orwell's dark vision, there was another - slightly older, slightly less well known, equally chilling: Aldous Huxley's *Brave New World.* Contrary to common belief even among the educated, Huxley and Orwell did not prophesy the same thing. Orwell warns that we will be overcome by an externally imposed oppression. But in Huxley's vision, no Big Brother is required to deprive people of their autonomy, maturity and history. As he saw it, people will come to love their oppression, to adore the technologies that undo their capacities to think.

What Orwell feared were those who would ban books. What Huxley feared was that there would be no reason to ban a book, for there would be no one who wanted to read one. Orwell feared those who would deprive us of information. Huxley feared those who would give us so much that we would be reduced to passivity and egoism. Orwell feared that the truth would be concealed from us. Huxley feared the truth would be drowned in a sea of irrelevance. Orwell feared we would become a captive culture. Huxley feared we would become a trivial culture, preoccupied with some equivalent of the feelies, the orgy porgy, and the centrifugal bumblepuppy. As Huxley remarked in Brave New World Revisited, the civil libertarians and rationalists who are ever on the alert to oppose tyranny "failed to take into account man's almost infinite appetite for distractions." In 1984, Orwell added, people are controlled by inflicting pain. In *Brave New World,* they are controlled by inflicting pleasure. In short, Orwell feared that what we fear will ruin us. Huxley feared that what we desire will ruin us.

This book is about the possibility that Huxley, not Orwell, was right."

Neil Postman, *Amusing Ourselves to Death: Public Discourse in the Age of Show Business.* Not brief; but good.

"Many people spend their lives in a job they hate, to earn money to buy things they don't need, to impress people they don't even like very much."

Caroline Kataria, my elder daughter, brought me this years ago. She had heard it during a TED talk. My best efforts on the search engines have not so far located an originator, so I continue to credit it to Caroline. And it remains my favourite argument for finding a job you love.

'THE LITERARY ENDEAVOUR'

"Better to write for yourself and have no public, than write for the public and have no self."

Cyril Connolly

"I don't think a book properly exists in the world until it's been translated into another language from its original."

Ali Smith. Not sure that I agree with this but Ms Smith is better qualified to have an opinion than am I.

"The most important thing for me is that I've used my talents as a writer to enable the Ogoni people to confront their tormentors. I was not able to do it as a politician or as a businessman. My writing did it."

Ken Saro-Wiwa

"Out of the quarrel with others we make rhetoric; out of the quarrel with ourselves we make poetry."

W B Yeats

“A good book is the essence of a human soul.”

Thomas Carlyle

“We who live by writing and publishing want and should demand our share of the proceeds; but the name of our beautiful reward isn’t profit. Its name is freedom.”

Ursula K Le Guin

“Writing can be encouraged perhaps, but taught? To teach something implies there is something to be taught and that suggests that the activity can be reduced to, if not rules, maxims. But there are no rules except to tell a story.”

Bernard Cornwell

“The task I set myself technically in writing a book from eighteen different points of view and in as many styles … would be enough to upset anyone’s mental balance.”

James Joyce, on writing *Ulysses*. Reading it has not done wonders for my mental balance.

"Painters have often taught writers how to see, and once you have had that experience you see differently."

James Baldwin

"One gains a double benefit in writing about the past, conjuring up how things might have been, and at the same time acquiring a different perspective on the present."

Robert Harris, who along with Hilary Mantel changed my view of historical fiction.

"Try to read your own work as a stranger would read it, or even better as an enemy would."

Zadie Smith

"Be regular and orderly in your life, so that you can be violent and original in your work."

Gustave Flaubert

"A thought is often original, though you have uttered it a hundred times. It has come to you over a new route, by a new and express train of associations."

Oliver Wendell Holmes

"I like the feeling of a fountain pen. I like uncapping it. I like the weight of it in my hand."

Neil Gaiman

"Writing non-fiction is more like sculpture, a matter of shaping the research into the finished thing."

Joan Didion

"When I want to read a novel, I write one."

Benjamin Disraeli

"Certainly one knows more at forty than one did at twenty. And contrary to all American mythology, the novel is the rightful province not of the young but of the middle-aged."

Gore Vidal

“Writing a novel is a terrible experience, during which the hair often falls out and the teeth decay. I’m always irritated by people who imply that writing fiction is an escape from reality. It is a plunge into reality and it’s very shocking to the system.”

Flannery O’Connor

“A novelist can do anything he wants so long as he makes people believe in it.”

Gabriel Garcia Marquez

“A good stylist should have a narcissistic enjoyment as he works. He must be able to objectivize his work to such an extent that he catches himself feeling envious. In short, he must display that highest degree of objectivity which the world calls vanity.”

Karl Kraus

“A good book is the precious life-blood of a master spirit, embalmed and treasured up on purpose to a life beyond life.”

John Milton

“A well chosen anthology is a complete dispensary of medicine for the more common mental disorders, and may be used as much for prevention as for cure.”

Robert Graves, to whom my thanks for supporting the cause of anthologies.

“We all know that books burn. Yet we have the greater knowledge that books cannot be killed by fire. People die but books never die. No man and no force can abolish memory. In this war, as we know, books are weapons.”

President Franklin D Roosevelt, in 1942. Powerful words.

“A widely-read man never quotes accurately. Misquotation is the pride and privilege of the learned.”

Hesketh Pearson. So if any of the entries in this volume are misquotations, I rest my case.

“The very existence of libraries affords the best evidence that we may yet have hope for the future of man.”

T S Eliot

"Civilised nations build libraries."

John Major

"There are many reasons why novelists write but they have one thing in common: a need to create an imaginary world."

John Fowles

"I don't think writers choose the genre, the genre chooses us. I wrote out of the wish to create order out of disorder, the liking of a pattern."

P D James

Don't shove me into your damn pigeonhole, where I don't fit, because I'm all over. My tentacles are coming out of the pigeonhole in all directions."

Ursula K Le Guin

“What is writing a novel like? The beginning: a ride through a spring wood. The middle: the Gobi desert. The end: going down the Cresta run. I am now (p.166 of *The Buccaneers*) in the middle of the Gobi desert.”

Edith Wharton

“Exercising is a good analogy for writing. If you’re not used to exercising you want to avoid it forever.”

Jennifer Egan

“Poetry is the spontaneous overflow of powerful feelings. It takes its origin from emotion recollected in tranquillity.”

William Wordsworth

“Whom the gods wish to destroy they first call promising.”

Cyril Connolly

"And yet, the only exciting life is the imaginary one."

Virginia Woolf

“What have I gained by health? Intolerable dullness. What by early hours and moderate meals? A total blank.”

Charles Lamb

“I may write garbage but you can always edit garbage. You can’t edit a blank page.”

Jodi Picoult

“Substitute ‘damn’ every time you’re inclined to write ‘very.’ Your editor will delete it and the writing will be just as it should be.”

Mark Twain

“Read over your compositions, and where ever you meet with a passage that you think is particularly fine, strike it out.”

Samuel Johnson

“There is no point trying to analyse the creative urge. You either have it or you don’t.”

David Hewson

“A creative life is more a scavenger hunt, following a trail of breadcrumbs, than it is lightning in a bottle.”

Elizabeth Gilbert

“Becoming a writer is not a ‘career decision’ like becoming a doctor or a policeman. You don’t choose it as much as get chosen, and you have to be prepared to walk a long, hard road for the rest of your days.”

Paul Auster. Wow.

“I believe writers are writers the day they describe themselves as such.”

Adele Parks

“For a true writer each book should be a new beginning where he tries again for something that is beyond attainment.”

Ernest Hemingway

"There is something delicious about writing the first words of a story. You never know where they'll take you."

Beatrix Potter

"… remember that in the particularity of your own life lies the seed-corn that will feed your imaginative work. So don't throw it all away on autobiography. (There are quite enough writers' memoirs out there already.)

Rose Tremain. *Ten rules for writing fiction, Part 2.*

"Literature is also a curiously intimate way of communicating with people you will never meet."

Julian Barnes. From Shusha Guppy: *Julian Barnes, the art of fiction no. 165*. Mr Barnes nails it again.

"Some writers confuse authenticity, which they ought always to aim at, with originality, which they should never bother with."

W H Auden, *The Dyer's Hand.*

“I will not have in my writing any elegance, effect or originality – to hang in the way between me and the rest like curtains … what I tell I tell for precisely what it is.”

Walt Whitman, *Preface to Leaves of Grass.*

"Literature is strewn with the wreckage of those who have minded beyond reason the opinion of others."

Virginia Woolf, *A Room of One's Own.*

"I have a deeply hidden and inarticulate desire for something beyond the daily life."

Virginia Woolf, *Moments of Being: A Collection of Autobiographical Writing.*

"You light up the world. You can't help it."

Fanny Ronalds to Sir Arthur Sullivan. What a wonderful compliment to pay someone! To which I add "May that be truly said of us, and all of us." (From *A Christmas Carol*, by Dickens, albeit in a different context.)

The source of this compliment was the screenplay of the film *Topsy-Turvy,* which ends with the triumphant opening night of Gilbert & Sullivan's then-new comic opera *The Mikado.*

Mary Frances 'Fanny' Ronalds was not a fictional creation for the purpose of the film but a noted beauty and American socialite who had a long-standing relationship with Sullivan. He described her as the best amateur singer in London and she was famously associated with one of Sullivan's most popular songs, *The Lost Chord.*

"Writing is like being in love. You never get better at it or learn more about it. The day you think you do is the day you lose it. Robert Frost called his work a lover's quarrel with the world. It's ongoing. It has neither a beginning nor an end. You don't have to worry about learning things. The fire of one's art burns all the impurities from the vessel that contains it."

James Lee Burke

"We don't read and write poetry because it's cute. We read and write poetry because we are members of the human race. And the human race is filled with passion. So medicine, law, business, engineering... these are noble pursuits and necessary to sustain life. But poetry, beauty, romance, love... these are what we stay alive for."

Walt Whitman, *Leaves of Grass.*

"I read so I can live more than one life in more than one place."

Anne Tyler

"Literature duplicates the experience of living in a way that nothing else can, drawing you so fully into another life that you temporarily forget you have one of your own. That is why you read it, and might even sit up in bed till early dawn, throwing your whole tomorrow out of whack, simply to find out what happens to some people who, you know perfectly well, are made up."

Barbara Kingsolver. I'd never read any of her books until I came across what she has written about the process of writing. I was so impressed, I started to read her novels too, beginning with *The Bean Trees.*

“Don't try to figure out what other people want to hear from you; figure out what you have to say.”

Barbara Kingsolver. I think she’s said this more than once in different words, so it’s a fair bet that she believes it. Good advice, I believe.

“I learned to write by reading the kind of books I wished I'd written.”

Barbara Kingsolver

“God bless the Reference Librarians”

James Lee Burke. Who then expanded the thought, as follows:

"I long ago became convinced that the most reliable source for arcane and obscure and seemingly unobtainable information does not lie with the government or law enforcement agencies. Apparently neither the CIA nor the military intelligence apparatus inside the Pentagon had even a slight inkling of the Soviet Union's impending collapse, right up to the moment the Kremlin's leaders were trying to cut deals for their memoirs with New York publishers. Or, if a person really wishes a lesson in the subjective nature of official information, he can always call the IRS and ask for help with his tax forms, then call back a half hour later and ask the same questions to a different representative. So where do you go to find a researcher who is intelligent, imaginative, skilled in the use of computers, devoted to discovering the truth, and knowledgeable about science, technology, history, and literature, and who usually works for dirt and gets credit for nothing? After lunch I drove to the city library on Main and asked the reference librarian to find what she could on Junior Crudup."

James Lee Burke, *Last Car to Elysian Fields.* The wonderful Burke has more than once praised reference librarians, so I make no apology if I've been guilty of repetition. I only add a shout-out, as we say in the trade, to my former neighbour the late Mike Davies: a truly cultured man who first told me how good James Lee Burke's books were. I thank Mike every time I read anything from Burke's massive output.

"Humility is not a virtue in a writer, it is an absolute necessity."

James Lee Burke

"And every good artist knows that the gift comes from somewhere else, and it's there for a reason, and that's to make the world a better place."

James Lee Burke. A crime writer who truly wants to make the world a better place.

"Don't give up. I don't think any other advice works. Writing is one of those things where you just have to do it. There will be far more people to discourage you than to encourage you. The time never comes to you, the inspiration doesn't come to you. You just sit down and do it."

James Lee Burke, quoted in James Scott Bell's *How to Make a Living As a Writer.*

"You do it a day at a time. You write as well as you can, you put it in the mail, you leave it under submission, you never leave it at home."

James Lee Burke, *quoted by J.R. Lindermuth.*

"Thinking at night isn't good for anybody."

James Lee Burke, *House of the Rising Sun.* I'm so glad to have had my own findings confirmed by this king of contemporary crime.

"Never underestimate the vital importance of finding early in life the work that for you is play. This turns possible underachievers into happy warriors."

Ken Robinson, *The Element: How Finding Your Passion Changes Everything.*

"Eighty percent of success is showing up."

Woody Allen

"We don't read and write poetry because it's cute. We read and write poetry because we are members of the human race. And the human race is filled with passion. So medicine, law, business, engineering... these are noble pursuits and necessary to sustain life. But poetry, beauty, romance, love... these are what we stay alive for."

Walt Whitman, *Leaves of Grass.*

"Determine never to be idle. No person will have occasion to complain of the want of time, who never loses any. It is wonderful how much may be done, if we are always doing."

Thomas Jefferson, *Letters of Thomas Jefferson.* I hereby resolve to avoid wasting time. I'll let you know how that goes.

"What do I miss, as a human being, if I have never heard of the Second Law of Thermodynamics? The answer is: Nothing. And what do I miss by not knowing Shakespeare? Unless I get my understanding from another source, I simply miss my life. Shall we tell our children that one thing is as good as another-- here a bit of knowledge of physics, and there a bit of knowledge of literature? If we do so, the sins of the fathers will be visited upon the children unto the third and fourth generation, because that normally is the time it takes from the birth of an idea to its full maturity when it fills the minds of a new generation and makes them think by it. Science cannot produce ideas by which we could live."

E.F. Schumacher, *Small Is Beautiful: Economics as if People Mattered.* This stopped me in my tracks, as a large chunk of my own life has been dominated by a scientific education and the career into which it led me.

"The only reward to be expected from the cultivation of literature is contempt if one fails and hatred if one succeeds."

Voltaire

“Literature, not scripture, sustains the mind and—since there is no other metaphor—also the soul.”

Christopher Hitchens

“Nobody made a greater mistake than he who did nothing because he could do only a little.”

Edmund Burke. I’d say this is a good message for anyone engaged in a creative enterprise. Or any enterprise, in fact.

“I do not know what I think until I write it.”

George Bernard Shaw. This has been my watchword for years.

“The headmaster of my primary school said I was fated to become a writer. Doomed might have been a better word.”

My novelist friend **John Lynch**, who was kind enough to write the Forewords to both Volume 1 of this series and to my earlier *Wedding Speech Handbook.*

"Only in books has mankind known perfect truth, love and beauty."

George Bernard Shaw

"The plain working truth is that it is not only good for people to be shocked occasionally, but absolutely necessary to the progress of society that they should be shocked pretty often."

George Bernard Shaw, *The Quintessence of Ibsenism.*

WIT AND WISDOM

"This is not a novel to be tossed aside lightly. It should be thrown with great force."

Dorothy Parker

"Wit ought to be a glorious treat like caviar; never spread it around like marmalade."

Noel Coward

"If you are in difficulties with a book, try the element of surprise: attack it at an hour when it isn't expecting it."

H G Wells. I didn't know Wells had a sense of humour; now I do.

"It is a sad fact about our culture that a poet can earn much more money writing or talking about his art than he can by practising it."

W H Auden. I shall pass copies of this to my poet friends.

"I keep them (three typewriters) chiefly to remind myself that I was once a writer."

Dashiell Hammett

"It is not enough to succeed. Others must fail."

Gore Vidal

"To give an accurate and exhaustive account of that period would require a far less brilliant pen than mine."

Max Beerbohm

"The original is unfaithful to the translation."

Jorge Luis Borges

"If you like my novels, I commend your good taste."

Rita Mae Brown

"I don't read novels whilst I'm writing one. I just haven't got a wide enough brain to concentrate on incoming and outgoing in the same time zone."

Dawn French

"A conversation is a dialogue, not a monologue. That's why there are so few good conversations: due to scarcity, two intelligent talkers seldom meet."

Truman Capote

"It usually takes me more than three weeks to prepare a good impromptu speech."

Mark Twain. I think I used this in my earlier book *The Wedding Speech Handbook.* What a gift it is to make a speech seem as fresh as if all the thoughts are newly minted.

"Mark Twain and I are in the same position. We have to put things in such a way as to make people, who would otherwise hang us, believe that we are joking."

George Bernard Shaw

"No poet or novelist wishes he were the only one who ever lived but most of them wish they were the only one alive; and quite a number fondly believe their wish has been granted."

W H Auden

"Writing is a way of talking without being interrupted."

Jules Renard

"I know I was writing stories when I was five. I don't know what I did before that. Just loafed, I suppose."

P G Wodehouse

"Has anybody ever seen a dramatic critic in the daytime? Of course not. They come out after dark, up to no good."

P G Wodehouse

"From the moment I picked up your book until I laid it down, I was convulsed with laughter. Some day I intend reading it."

Groucho Marx

"Drama is the back-stairs of the intellect. Philosophers and historians go in by the front door but playwrights and novelists sneak up the back stairs with their more disreputable luggage."

Alan Bennett

"I must have a prodigious quantity of mind; it takes me as much as a week, sometimes, to make it up."

Mark Twain

"Humour is the first of the gifts to perish in a foreign tongue."

Virginia Woolf

"Everywhere I go I'm asked if I think the university stifles writers. My opinion is that they don't stifle enough of them. There's many a best-seller that could have been prevented by a good teacher."

Flannery O'Connor

"He thought her beautiful, believed her impeccably wise; dreamed of her, wrote poems to her, which, ignoring the subject, she corrected in red ink."

Virginia Woolf, *Mrs. Dalloway.*

"Muriel Spark is said to have felt that she was taking dictation from God every morning—sitting there, one supposes, plugged into a Dictaphone, typing away, humming. But this is a very hostile and aggressive position. One might hope for bad things to rain down on a person like this."

Anne Lamott, *Bird by Bird: Instructions on Writing and Life.*

"The story is told. I think I now see the judicious reader putting on his spectacles to look for the moral. It would be an insult to his sagacity to offer directions. I only say, God speed him in his quest!"

Charlotte Brontë, *Shirley.* I've never read that novel, so my thanks are due to David Lodge who used the quotation as a preface to Part 4 of his novel *Nice Work.*

"If you think … that anything like a romance is preparing for you, reader, you were never more mistaken. Do you anticipate sentiment, and poetry, and reverie? Do you expect passion, and stimulus, and melodrama? Calm your expectations, reduce them to a lowly standard. Something real, cool and solid lies before you; something as unromantic as Monday morning, when all who have work wake with the consciousness that they must rise and betake themselves thereto."

Charlotte Brontë, Prelude to *Shirley*. My thanks are due again to David Lodge, who used this quotation as an introduction to his 1988 novel *Nice Work*, which was also about 'Monday mornings'.

"The only thing standing between me and greatness is me."

Woody Allen

"The only reward to be expected from the cultivation of literature is contempt if one fails and hatred if one succeeds."

Voltaire

“Women read men more truly than men read women. I’ll prove that in a magazine paper some day when I have time; only it will never be inserted. It will be ‘declined with thanks,’ and left for me at the publisher’s.”

Charlotte Brontë

“The governor of Texas, when asked if the Bible should also be taught in Spanish, replied: ‘if English was good enough for Jesus, then it’s good enough for me’.”

Christopher Hitchens, one of my heroes. However, I don’t plan to retell this story next time I have a speaking engagement in Texas.

“My main reason for adopting literature as a profession was that, as the author is never seen by his clients, he need not dress respectably.”

George Bernard Shaw

“When a thing is funny, search it carefully for a hidden truth.”

George Bernard Shaw, *Back to Methuselah*. I love this.

"There is nothing in the world so irresistibly contagious as laughter and good humour."

Charles Dickens, *A Christmas Carol.*

"England and America are two countries separated by a common language."

George Bernard Shaw. You thought that Churchill said this first? Me too. Or Oscar Wilde? Me too.

"Had my books been any worse I would not have been invited to Hollywood and if they had been any better I would not have come."

Raymond Chandler

WORDS, WORDS, WORDS

"[Libraries are] safe, warm places where anyone can learn to read, to dream, to use English, sometimes, or a computer. Or, perhaps, to be a writer."

Maggie Gee

"I shouldn't complain, but really, I have too many ideas. They line up like urgent spectres shouting 'me, me!' until I give in and beckon one of them to the head of the queue."

Emma Donoghue

"Do change your mind. Good ideas are often murdered by better ones."

Roddy Doyle

"When I split an infinitive, god damn it, I split it so it stays split."

Raymond Chandler

"Writing is an act of faith, not a trick of grammar."

E B White

"Due attention to the inside of books, and due contempt for the outside, is the proper relation between a man of sense and his books."

Philip, Lord Stanhope, *Letters to his son.* Is he saying that the words are the only thing that matters? If so, many of us today would cheer, as we anguish over cover designs and all the rest. But I suppose in 18th-centrury England one's competition didn't bother about cover designs either.

"I feel sorry for novelists when they have to mention women's eyes: there's so little choice, and whatever colouring is decided upon inevitably carries banal implications. Her eyes are blue: innocence and honesty. Her eyes are black: passion and depth. Her eyes are green: wildness and jealousy. Her eyes are violet: the novel is by Raymond Chandler."

Julian Barnes, *Flaubert's Parrot.* Barnes referencing Chandler represents a double pleasure for me.

"Technique alone is never enough. You have to have passion. Technique alone is just an embroidered potholder."

Raymond Chandler. Not sure what a potholder is but otherwise I like this.

P.S. Two weeks before this book went to press I visited *The Titanic Experience* at Cobh in the south of Ireland (formerly named Queenstown) the Titanic's last port of call, and there I saw a potholder. It was a thing for holding pots.

"There was a sad fellow over on a bar stool talking to the bartender, who was polishing a glass and listening with that plastic smile people wear when they are trying not to scream."

Raymond Chandler, *The Long Goodbye.* I put this here for that last clause.

"Everything a writer learns about the art or craft of fiction takes just a little away from his need or desire to write at all. In the end he knows all of the tricks and has nothing to say."

Raymond Chandler

"The faster I write the better my output. If I'm going slow, I'm in trouble. It means I'm pushing the words instead of being pulled by them."

Raymond Chandler

"They were like people who run to meet, holding out their arms, but their aim is wrong; they pass each other and keep running."

Anne Tyler. I love this; but I don't know if it came from a novel, or was something she said in an interview, or whatever: I usually like to find that out. But does it matter? There's a point of view that what a novelist says through one of his or her characters is the unvarnished, unmediated truth of that author's attitude. "Discuss", as my teachers used to say.

WORK ETHIC

"Neglect everything else."

David Mitchell (the novelist, not the comedian), on writing. One day I will tell you I have lived up to this exhortation; but I'm not there yet.

"No task is a long one but the task which one dare not start. It becomes a nightmare."

Charles Baudelaire

"It is not real work unless you would rather be doing something else."

J M Barrie

"People say that perfectionism is bad. But it's because of perfectionists that man walked on the moon and painted the Sistine Chapel, OK? Perfectionism is good."

Donna Tartt

"Be regular and orderly in your life, so that you can be violent and original in your work."

Gustave Flaubert

"Abandon the idea that you're ever going to finish. Lose track of the 400 pages and write just one page for each day; it helps."

John Steinbeck

"If you write one story, it may be bad. If you write a hundred, you have the odds in your favour."

Edgar Rice Burroughs

"The most important virtue for a writer, I believe, is self-forgiveness. Because your writing will always disappoint you. Your laziness will always disappoint you."

Elizabeth Gilbert

"I act as a sponge. I soak it up and squeeze it out in ink every two weeks."

Janet Flanner, Paris correspondent of *The New Yorker*.

"Good novels are produced by people who voluntarily isolate themselves, and go deep, and report from the depths on what they find."

Jonathan Frantzen

"I don't think necessity is the mother of invention. Invention, in my opinion, arises directly from idleness, possibly also from laziness. To save oneself trouble."

Agatha Christie

"When I am in the country I wish to vegetate like the country."

William Hazlitt

"It is impossible to enjoy idling thoroughly unless one has plenty of work to do."

Jerome K Jerome

"Time enough to think and cut and rewrite tomorrow. But today-explode-fly-apart-disintegrate! The other six or seven drafts are going to be pure torture. So why not enjoy the first draft, in the hope that your joy will seek and find others who, by reading your story, will catch fire too?"

Ray Bradbury. Brief this isn't; but it is Ray Bradbury, who writes so well on the craft of writing. And of course that phrase 'catch fire' is perfect, coming from the author of *Fahrenheit 451*. I'm glad he slipped that in.

"The artistic impulse seems not to wish to produce finished work. It certainly deserts us halfway, after the idea is born; and if we go on, all art is labour."

Clarence Shepard Day

"The road to hell is paved with work-in-progress."

Philip Roth

"Sit myself in my chair and threaten myself like a recalcitrant child: you will sit in this chair and you will not move until you get this scene written, missy."

Gillian Flynn

“An artist cannot do anything slovenly.”

Jane Austen, *from a letter to her sister Cassandra*

“You have to be efficient if you’re going to be lazy.”

Shirley Conran

“The one ironclad rule is that I have to try. I have to walk into my writing room and pick up my pen every weekday morning.”

Anne Tyler. Clearly she’s done more than try, to judge by her output.

“If I waited till I felt like writing, I'd never write at all.”

Anne Tyler

“I have yet to meet a writer who wouldn’t rather peel a banana than apply himself to the pen.”

Alice Thomas Ellis. I have a rule about including almost anything written by Ms Ellis, real name Anna Lindholm.

“The fact is, writing can be done only during the hours when one ought be be doing something else.”

Isabel Paterson

“If you have a burning, restless urge to write or paint, simply eat something sweet and the feeling will pass.”

Fran Lebowitz, with advice for all my super-assiduous writer friends.

“I have the suspicion that excessive literary production is a social offence.”

George Eliot. Anything by the wonderful Ms Evans has to be included in this book. I suppose that if one could have produced work of her quality, excessive quantity would be unnecessary.

“Beavers try too hard. If they were less industrious, they’d be a protected species.”

Chris Bonington

"An amateur... has a million plans and they all start tomorrow."

Stephen Pressfield, *Do the Work.*

"You have to work with what God sends and if God doesn't understand the concept of commercial success, then that's your bad luck."

Michael Frayn, on writing. I used this in the 'Lady Luck' section of an earlier volume of this series. Even if hard work beats luck, the latter has an influence far above our expectations. Call it serendipity if you like: I never cease to be amazed at the stories people tell me of the influence of luck on their lives.

WRITER'S BLOCK

"If I'm stuck with a particular chapter or part of my book, I have been known to buy a return ticket, jump on a train and write."

Malorie Blackman

"I write very small, so I don't have to turn the page and face the next empty one."

Michael Morpurgo

QUOTATIONS ABOUT QUOTATIONS

… which seems a good way to close this book.

"Brevity is the soul of wit."

William Shakespeare, *Hamlet.* My title: and a principle which is contradicted by some of the longer maxims in these volumes but remains valid nonetheless.

"It is a good thing for an uneducated man to read books of quotations. *Bartlett's Familiar Quotations* is an admirable work, and I studied it intently. The quotations when engraved upon the memory give you good thoughts. They also make you anxious to read the authors and look for more."

Winston Churchill, *My Early Life.* Even if he was, at the time, scornful about quotations and how they can help 'an uneducated man', it turns out that he's the source, or the claimed source, of half of the quotations ever published.

"The only way to read a book of aphorisms without being bored is to open it at random and, having found something that interests you, close the book and meditate."

Prince de Ligne, *Mes Ecarts.*

"Good things, when short, are twice as good."

Baltasar Gracian, *The Art of Worldly Wisdom.*

"It is my ambition to say in ten sentences what other men say in whole books – what other men do not say in whole books."

Friedrich Nietzsche, *Twilight of the Idols.*

"Men's maxims reveal their characters."

Luc de Clapiers, Marquis de Vauvenargues, *Reflections and Maxims.*

"There are things which don't deserve to be said briefly."

Jean Rostand, *De la vanite.* Another contradiction of the purpose of this series. But I decided to proceed with the project anyway. I hope you have enjoyed the result.

"Everything that needed to be said has already been said. But because nobody was listening, it has to be said again."

Andre Gide. My favourite on the subject.

AND FINALLY …

I hope you've enjoyed this miscellany.

If you could take a few minutes to post a review I'd appreciate it.

We authors value feedback, whether positive or negative!

Michael J MacMahon

Printed in Great Britain
by Amazon

21228690R00081